T0086081

SOLILOQUY WITH THE GHOSTS IN NILE

Hussain Ahmed

Black Ocean
Boston · Chicago

Black Ocean
P.O. Box 52030
Boston, MA 02205
blackocean.org

ISBN: 978-1-939568-52-6

Library of Congress Control Number: 2022933040
Printed in Canada

FIRST EDITION

CONTENTS

For the twelve stars, and the sun, and the two moons—
I prostrate to them all

I

GENESIS

If a new life begins after each blackout,
all the ghosts in this house would have to wake
from their slumbers. The last man
steps out of the makabarta
and it seems like learning jazz again.
Each time
we walk into the boneyard
with stereos muffled in our stomachs.
The path of dust
in between the graves   lead
to another freshly dug hole, a space for a new beginning.
Cairns erected
over new heaps of brown soil,
only a few had epitaphs,   I assume
none of their lovers found a tongue   to fill the cabinets
with a song   that'll round off the edges of their emptiness.
This, like the night   when thunder
unbuttoned the sky, to give space for the wandering shadows,
I feel my bones reverse to be tendons again.
On the grave marker, I see names that sound too close to mine
and dates as close   as the day before.
A piece of her bedsheet was wrapped around her marker
as if to remind us all
that   only the living should crave warmth,
because the sky has never been closer

no matter how high we jump.
Here, the gates are opened for goats
to wander and graze upon all that grows
for staying long beneath the ground.
I see taro leaves   sprouting
from the plain ground, waiting to be dug.
The last man steps out of the makabarta,
this time,   he looks behind—
a bird perched on the new marker.
How long
until another will be planted?
How long
does any part of the graveyard remain plain
until it becomes a new country?

FLIGHT

The day an airplane crashed,
the air became heavy
with the aura of mouths
sore with grieving songs.
I was taught to plead with the fire in my broken tongue
as would an owl, tired of nocturne.
Today, we celebrate everyone
that died in flight,
everyone who had a name
similar to ours.
I felt all our dead reincarnated in me today,
my body is now soundproof;
I do not recognize the songs that slip out of my mouth.

HOW THE WAR MADE US A NAME

Before the war, we had names we inherited
from the dead. They keep us warm
until we start to lose those names to the wind.

The long corridors in my throat are of tinted glass windows,
all that happened belongs in the darkness
of what may wash off the memories of all the dead.

I wake up with scars on my arms, and it surprises me
that I still feel dead after gulping a cup of pap.
I feel strange in my father's frock too,

even though it keeps me warm. I need
all the heat I can get today, so the eggs in my body
can hatch and be set free to make nests

far from here, where they would not be hunted
to deliver obituaries in envelopes that are large enough
to be registers, wherein our names are written

for each condolence visit. The war made us names
too much to keep up with. We learn to escape the burning
before we learn that every name we inherit comes with allergies.

I threw a harp inside the fireplace, and it poured out the tunes
I once heard baba play on it. It stopped when it got swallowed
in the flames—all we inherited still burns.

APERTURE DIAMETER

On the walls were hieroglyphs around the paintings of bison. Down the cave, the names of executed prisoners were etched

with fingernails or broken teeth. The embers in his eyes glowed but did not die out, even though his tears washed his irises to ashes.

In the corridor of a cinema, I imagined soldiers rammed their feet in his chest as if to render him heartless, or to purge him of what belonged to the friends they lost

to the fog in Sambisa, or the roadblock that's also a graveyard. He was arrested a few meters away from home and labeled a terrorist because he looked like my father.

I tried to blink my eyes, to unshackle this vision for I feared I would become a desert if I let go of all the water in my eyes. This is the closest I had been to a ghost.

I watched smoke coiled towards the sky, it could be anyone's house. I didn't get to choose how far it could go until it disappeared among the moist embrace of the clouds.

This memory played in my mind, but the darkness rendered me unstable. I am driving backward, the soldiers moved away from my car, and soon, their khaki fades.

REVERSE CONCERT

Sing,
of the pyramid of ruins that is left of home.
Before the fire, this house was an aquarium,
transparent—only from inside.
We are surrounded by walls of brown paper
that are also maps of countries we visit in sleep.
The degrees inside the room coincide
with the weather outside. All my aunties are in matching gowns,
patterned like the flowers in the vase.
About home I sing, without telling of what whispers I heard in the wind.
I was betrayed by my own tongue; it learned to sing in other languages.
This tongue is a stem in a vasculum or a flower blackened by soot.
I left home before the fire, but I still blame the fire for my scars.
To run around in circles is the easiest way to undo the burning.
From here, it's difficult to tell what direction a bead rolls around a ring.
To unmake the fire, I become too young for the dance floor.
In my palms are the seeds saved from the fire,
It is all I can will to my unborn children, even though what we own
drown us with its weight, I find it hard to unclench my fist,
or stop to sing.

HOW TO PRAY FOR A BIRD IN FLIGHT

My baba teaches me to talk to God.
I fold my arms around my body
to show how cold I stand in a jellabiya.

I've had the same shadow for too long
and it does not hide me from the sun.

The gravediggers lower another girl into the earth.
We thank them [again] and we give sadaqah
and label the grave plate in bold letters.

My baba teaches me to pray for my dead sisters,
they survived the war and the curfew, but died

months after, in a labor room. I don't keep dates of my losses
even though my stomach is cold enough to preserve my griefs.

I pray that a gazebo will not be made of my bones.
The scar on my leg is evidence that I was born a cartographer.

This is the closest I am to a bird, and maybe to God.

CURFEW

1. My body was colonized / in a language of silence. / Strands of
   my hair entrapped the ghosts in the wind. / They were not held
   prisoner / but the abrasions kept them warm—or stuck. /

2. The sky was void of stars / or the smoke hid them from us. / We
   became satellites to each other / our shadows orbited our bodies
   from distance / until they became entangled. /

3. We were planets of silences during the curfew / the stones in the
   fireplace were all we had to fill up our wounds / instead / we let
   houseflies sing around the openings.

4. Baba kept guard throughout those nights with his knife /
   sharpened with grief.

5. His body was a fireplace / or a mosque full of ashes. / We said our
   prayers silently—the soldiers slipped into the house / and stained
   the wall with semen. / All our children woke up with bloated
   stomachs. / The wall was blue of a raging sea / threatening to wash
   out the whole town. / We plucked out sponges from our tongues
   / and scrubbed the house clean / before we dressed our wounds
   with foreign flags.

6. All we inherited from father was saved in an ambulance. / The
   siren was muted but its blue light flickered in the night. / We got
   stuck on ruts of bones / now it's our turn to unpack the street /
   our turn to become the gravediggers. /

7. A date tree grows from Baba's grave. / We stand around it, but its shadow does not keep out the sun bites. / After the curfew, we got served shayi / to heal the sores in our mouths.

8. These scars are evidence that we mistake silence for peace.

DOCUMENTARY OF A BRIDE IN BAPTISM

The echoes in the wind   are the whimpering of ghosts
searching everywhere that burns   for warmth.

A well was dug inside a girl because we are at war,
and the thirst of the horses could not be quenched with maple syrup.

She kept counts of wounded men   that offered her hearts
rimmed with bullet holes.
She chose to remain silent about the dolphins in her stomach,

each of their fins was a fragment of stories   about men
that drowned   learning to grow gills because the air is filled
with smoke. She's a souvenir in her father's house. She grew light

anytime she closed her eyes   until the war ended
with music pouring down from the sky.

Layers of mascara   thickened her eyelashes.
To make a bride of her swollen orbs, a map was made of her face.

NOMENCLATURE

Species:

        Her hair grows into a flag and how long it flutters
        depends on whether it burns or not.

        There is a huge turret on her scalp,
        I wrapped my fingers around the trigger.

        My mother and I share the stories
        of women whose hair we've braided

        but are no longer here, to join in the rituals that make salt
        of our bodies, when everywhere was cold.

Genes:

        The blood that flows in our veins surged
        from a fountain that is also a confluence for strangers.

        It could be hard to convince anyone of the miles
        I dug into the ground to keep my tongue wet.

        The fossils of my fingernails should be enough proof
        that extinction begins with a single death and not a plague.

Family:
> A group of women seated in circles could be mistaken
> for a coven, and this too is how we lose our names.

> I was shown love when asked to dance in the rain—even though
> I'm dying of hypothermia; I am another form of civilization.

> The greatest love I had growing up in this house was to be
> thrown into the wild, to see how long it'll take to return.

Order:
> I have a compound eye, so I was named after my grandfather,
> and him after his grandfather.

> This house stays empty until we find another tenant
> that won't blame my cat for my cough.

> On the blue walls are 3D signs of Hamsa
> to keep the house safe from everything that flies.

Class:
> My body is a room packed with the rays of memories
> and the cupboards are filled to the brim with silent prayers.

> It all began as grub; until it could grow wings to fly because
> its flap is a form of song that escapes the reeds in my femur.

I hear vibrations from the mountain, and the sky outside is
now the color of my eyes when I'm pregnant with rage.

Phylum:

There is a historical language of how I got this dark skin,
it has nothing to do with how I could get shot, dancing
on my lawn at night.

The first law here states that I may be destroyed,
but could be made into shapes of aloe vera, growing
in a tin of sand.

Because mortality can translate to emptiness,
when my body floats, all that surrounds it swells
in the moisture it gains from the heat.

Incantations are a form of prayer when slurred slowly
same as when you look at the sky with so much empathy.

Kingdom:

This space is too empty to be filled with a mourning song.
The echoes are the first signs

that in my hair is a cage that housed fireflies,
bleeping to remind me of home.

I hear my voice intermittently when I sleep.
I dreamed that I float [face up] inside the well in the backyard.

It's 1929, and I'm in the same cell with the Aba women,
the scars on their cheeks are the language of rebellion against
patriarchy.

Domain:
      Here, we so much believe in miracles,
      I sight a new moon from the bowl of water.

      The second law of nomenclature states
      that I could lose my name at age twelve or younger.

      The circle of girls in the room
      found our voices to sing out our pains.

      We are more than a temple of griefs. Heat consumes our body
      and we lose all the water we had that kept us from burning.

Life:
      We live in a cell—I mean, the smallest form of life.
      We grow through the web until we lose our names.

      Revolution is how we get to lose
      all the griefs we inherited from all our dead.

      I tell my sick neighbor of how so much—the angels hate garlic
      and nakedness, I hung my nudes on her wall, but she died three
      days later—in her sleep.

If those stories about reincarnations are true, I don't understand
why we get pulled out of these bodies, as if we would germinate
inside the moon.

I am thinking again about what it means to be a flower,
the world wants me edible, but I won't be.

HUNGER

The brown lawn is an open wound sprayed with ointment /
it will bloom when it rains / mama washes all the utensils /
her veins throbbing on the sides of her neck / she tells me
Somalia is an amusement park/ her children get to laugh
only when they stand on parallel lines for food /
only then do they remember their tongues / she says
the sky is hungry / hundreds of angels are diagnosed with ulcers /
this country is full of stones in the wrong shapes /
      daisies are scarce
but funerals are cheap to come by / she says when stone ages /
it loses its firmness / The men are ready to drag their pants
above their navel to find the cure for hunger / a quest
reported in faint voices / around the date tree that had refused to die /
you said there is water for its taproot / there's water beneath our feet /
how deep do we have to dig? / we face the east in a single file /
in memory of the slain lambs whose blood did not quench our thirst /
the women murmured the names of their missing children /
      butterflies fluttered ·
around the seedless white grape / I heard the men shout amen in unison.

AFTERMATH

We dug the ground so many times
burying a dead body or sowing a seed
both of which did not grow.
Our griefs are colored as the soot
from a lantern gasping for fuel.
My neighbor gave birth when silence was all
that can be cherished like clean water
gushing out of the rusty mouth of the tap.
She was brave to have sealed the child's mouth
when he was not suckling her nipple.
Baba amends the house constitution,
we must punctuate every ten minutes with Ayatul Kursiyi
for protection. It must be in whispers.
This is how you know the people are tired of digging.
Our baba sits around a bonfire with the Peace Keepers.
Their hands cup their cheeks.
The sun creeps upon our dark faces.
Again, we excuse the intrusion.
Mama tells us to dance when we can,
it could be the last time we hear her sing.

REINCARNATION

The jinn that sits in mama's body is of a distant time zone.
She made tea in the night for all her unseen guests.

Her tongue was a deserted ranch where nothing edible could grow.
She said the sky would swallow us all if she doesn't keep guard.

Although our shadows can grow as tall as ten feet since we water them,
Mama's shadow stops growing because she stops sleeping at night.

We sought refuge in the barracks when she set our house on fire
or when the new angel in town was lynched to death. We panicked
and left the house.

All our windows opened, our sign of allegiance to the governance
of the land beyond the sky. I asked Mama what would happen
to the ghosts of all our dead

if they came home to find only the ruins of all that should remind them
that we say dua'a in their names. She said after the curfew, we will find a way
to build back our walls.

Curfew is our way of mourning all that could not be buried
because they turn to ashes in the fire. The debris suggests where it started
and it's not the kitchen.

I scribbled the names of all my dead aunties on the wall.
I listed their favorite fruits beside their names, with the thought
that nothing would ever change about them.

II

II

every death is an alley

—Yusef Komunyakaa

SATELLITE PHONE CALL AS A FORM
OF SUPPLICATION

I make supplications / to the birds whose feathers were blades / lost in war. / Birds whose bones could no longer be found / in the museum / because they flew over the face of the sky / in a time of climate change. / I come from a line of hunters / who did not wait for darkness to come / instead / they sing in the woods until a deer comes too close to the fire / and becomes frozen in the rays. / I make supplication to the owls that died in flight / love letters clipped between their beaks. / It never gets old to open my mouth / to show mama that I have her brown teeth. / She carries all her griefs with ease / like feathers on the butts of arrows traveling straight lines. / I make supplication to her hands / decorated with henna / though it loses its hue to the water during ablution. / I make supplication to the stitches on my mother's stomach. / It was the first sign that I was born to make a map / from the scars she inherited / from spreading her wings in the wind.

SATELLITE PHONE CALL TO THE BOYS
IN A FAULTY ARMOR TANK

Boys in their early teens hold pictures of their mothers in sweaty palms.

I should have been with them too, but they need someone here
to pick up their calls, when it seems God stopped checking the voicemail.

Before the phone rang, I had my eyeballs in water, but they softened—
and splintered into fingerlings. I hear their voices,
    asking me to make an ablution.

Today, I am a doctor in a ward full of dying hyacinths.
I hear them sing *"I bow before you and ask you to examine my heart today."*

I pray for the armor tank that should belong in the museum.
I pray for the museum that should hold beautiful things
    except for war relics.

I pray for all the relics that would have been prettier around the necks
    of a living soldier.
I pray for the soldier that would have been a painter

if there was no war that needed to be fought. I say these prayers aloud

into the telephone, until the line went back dead. I looked out the window,
the sky was like old cotton fabric, soaked in a hot bath of cornflowers.

SATELLITE PHONE CALL TO STRANGERS

I.

The chambers in my chest are crowded
with the ghosts of strangers that are also my lovers.

There is a girl that sings anytime it gets dark inside my body.
In return, I sing of an owl that never gets sore wings in flight.

II.

I filled the registers between the framed pictures,
flanked by shimmering candle lights.

It's cold, but mama asked that I leave the door open.
Today, even the stray cat will get a name.

A child was to meet Grandfather,
but that dream ended mid-flight.

III.

This body is a caravel of memories—not a bag of sand,
no matter how well it reflects in the sun.

Begin this way, the imam dropped his hands
to his sides, and he unsaid Allahu Akbar.

The waiting line for the burial thinned out.

IV.

An airplane landed six minutes after takeoff.

The hostesses smiled as they helped unbuckle
all the passengers before they alighted the airplane.

In the lounge, they reunited
with everyone who escorted them to the airport.

They waited for the announcements,
hours passed and there was none.

A hologram of coral skeletons projected on the wall.
& no one will miss the flight

that returns phoenixes to shredded eggshells,
instead of ashes. No one will mourn today.

SATELLITE PHONE CALL TO THE CHILD LEARNING TO DRAW HIS BABA'S FACE

He makes paintings
in his pajamas,

holding onto a brush
and singing praises of the sky.

A blurred image of a soldier hangs
on the white wall.

Baba smiles
in a gown with overflowing sleeves.

He stares at his reflection in a mirror,
but all he sees is a moon stained in blood.

He tries on his Baba's boots,
and mixes different shades of green

to paint the favorite picture of himself
in his baba's uniform.

SATELLITE PHONE CALL TO THE GARDENER
WHOSE MEMORY CAUGHT FIRE

The butterfly between her fingers stained her with its yellow.
A woman speaks to her spades, and she claims
she hears them speak back. Here, we call psychosis
by all its fancy names. We assume it would mean inheriting
a gene that requires our permission to inhibit what bloomed in
our absence. She had lost two sons to the sea and another two to bullets.
She wouldn't know which is deadlier—bullets or water.
In a ritual to the sky, she lights a candle inside a tumbler by the bedside.
On the day Baba left, she started to bury seeds
every month of his absence, to keep track of her memories
in her body, which loses more heat than it generates.
 I see her now, through the eyes of a raven, in a garden
that's also a diary. She forgets all else, but not the time
to bury a new seed. This was how she grew what had been lost
to water and bullets.

SATELLITE PHONE CALL TO GIRLS THAT WERE ONCE SAND MINERS

Without having to lose their tongues to gravity
in a pond of brown water, I see them wash mounds of earth
until they found Coltan. In the beginning, was a pond,
shallow—but it would be enough for baptism.
Their legs, ankle-deep in mud,
this is how they built a dam to keep their homes from burning,
but ended up breeding mosquitoes in the water.
Our homes are rings of minerals,
we become what we walk upon. Everything ends where it begins.
Mama has been sick for months,
but she complains the flowers in her body would die without the sun.
Anytime she sleeps with the lights on, she wakes up with smiles on her lips.
I am my mother with no flower to remediate the pains
of losing her lovers to the war. Mama begs that I don't dig
deeper than my knee. She tells me stories about her childhood
when the only time she dug the ground was to bury kernelled seeds
of sunflowers.

SATELLITE PHONE CALL TO THE PEACEKEEPERS

There are different spectrums of silence,
all of which originated from sign language.

Silence is a form of prayer,
but it's not enough to make you escape mourning.

The muezzins swallowed their tongues
so they did not get stained with the smoke in the air.

The minarets were castles of ghosts after the new millennium.
We prayed in our rooms for the weeks that followed.

The soldiers marched on our empty streets.
Their steps were whispers of incantations.

Red strings hang on the butt of their guns.
It shows they are entropies of solitude

in a body that's also a confluence of ghosts in uniforms.
We praised them in repeating soprano patterns when we heard gun-
    shots.

The avocado tree was set on fire to keep us warm.
All the fruits were buried in the ashes, and they ripened by sunrise.

The girls woke up with stains on their skirts.
In the phone booth, we asked that a call be placed to the lighthouse,

where the ghosts of our dead gather to keep the water warm.
We raised our voices until our lips ripped.

We paid the price of chaos with our blood,
for the girls are now diaries of a war that held us

in-between the wavelength of silence and peace,
in a town full of distant echoes.

SATELLITE PHONE CALL TO THE TOURISTS IN THE TRAIN STATION

I.

There are a thousand ways to make fire because the sea recedes
back into its skeleton—each day, it becomes farther from us.

How often do you dream of home when it begins to burn?
I supplicate to the sun to dry out my skin until it turns fireproof.

The branches of what grows on the train tracks when it rains
are curved arrowheads— shaped like cactuses.

The plants are faded hue of blood that stained the ground.

II.

I was born a few days before a giant fire in Kaduna.

It is safe to say I was bred for falconry; always ready for flight.
In the direction of Gabas, I journeyed until I found other tourists.

The train station is a purgatory of hope. I come here often
to tell strangers what I missed about my country.

III.

Cemeteries and train stations have in common the incisions
of the past that refused my memory its flicker of solitude.

I left home in search of a name and became a tourist of borders.
No matter how unsafe home is, I won't identify as an alien.

WI-FI IN A CEMETERY

When they found him, he was without his eyes.
There is a need for free Wi-Fi   in all
the cemeteries across this country.
Every day, a dead man is assumed on a journey,
and nobody wants to check their friends
where only ashes   could be found.
I lost a friend one Eid,
we cheered as he dove into the river.
Today, history is our enemy
with spears and spades in place of forks and spoons.
I stare at my phone, expecting a call from my drowned friend.
We sit on a bench   wrapped in the blooming fragrance of despair,
expectant of a miracle, and a verse of the Qur'an to calm the fire
that comes with prophecies.
We are yet to master the art of mourning, so no one cries.
Praise the sky, for how well it mourns.
We rehearsed how to break the news when we get home.
That day, we became men with bibs under our chins.
We folded the grief in our pockets. The news got to his mama
before we got home. I still expect an angel to knock on our door,
before the pain slips away, before we decide who wears his clothes.

HALOGEN

Each time we got displaced from home, we gained electrons
that brought back memories of how we sat around a dining table,

before the first blast that ushered the war.
Here, we substituted remedies for miracles.

[Fluorine]

We became products of salt when we remembered all that happened
to the table and the empty chairs that surrounded it.

I imagined our curtains were soaked in organobromine
because they repelled the flames from the pictures on the wall.

I isolated my body from her histories
and the nomenclature of the griefs buried within.

[Chlorine]

Displacements of oxygen made our lungs a garden of thorns. We know
there should be light far ahead, but it could also be another fire.

The pool prepared us for survival, but it wasn't enough—
it hurts to see my reflection in the blue water.

[Bromine]

There was word a new witch was going to be in town.
This was supposed to be a small congregation of mourners

as choristers. We imagined that our dead were on a journey
to discover new elements that could replace the salt in our jugs.

We all have loss in common. We have a body riddled with holes
that could also be a cellar with empty wine bottles filled with obituaries.

[Iodine]

    Today, the sky is blue-black, that's enough evidence
    for why the rain had our footprints erased.

    On the walls are stories of the girls that were here
    long before we ran out of vaccines.

    In my dreams, a pond of fingerlings turns into crabs anytime
       there's a full moon.
    I see my reflection on the wall, I am inches taller.

    I thought the world would be at peace if we all fell asleep at once,
    so I closed my eyes. When the smoke lost all its feathers,
    we became silent.

[Astatine]

Ten years after, mustards had grown from the decay of all we left
behind. It had our blood in its vines, but it looks dark as semiconductors.

The broken windows are enough evidence that we once lived
in ruins. The classroom is full of flowers, metaphors for the isotopes of red.

The leaves grew radiant in our absences,
and here we are, learning to walk in our new blouses.

[Undiscovered]

WI-FI IN A PRISON YARD

I tear up my heart into wigs of slivers
that I may remember how it all began.

There was an eclipse, and I misplaced my eyes
in the blood of the moon,
      a miscarriage of everything I owned.

I am sick of the nostalgia that comes with a stale memory
for what I should have seen,   before the darkness.

We find connections on the lines on our palms
      and it becomes entangled
in edible nests,   until a new inmate begins to cry.

This globe is full of darkness
and only the lit places are burning.

The fire punctured the ozone that blankets the verdin in my rib cage.
My heart is a wick of card sliver,   it spins in a pool of grief.

III

III

each god is empty without us

—Rita Dove

SOLILOQUY WITH THE GHOST IN NILE

The sky yesterday is no different from any day after it loses another star.
I lost a seedling to the soil in the season of ghosts, in Kakuri.

The women held their hands in prayer inside the ward, on their rosaries
were the names of Allah that borders *Al-Mumit*.

We all became light in our loose blouses, not ready to plant another. We
let our voices grow wings. There is no beauty in a prayer that's wingless.

The girl's body was filled with holes—like a deserted mining site.

She needs us to bury our rings and bracelets in the openings. But that
could be another form of proposing to the ghosts in her wounds.

How do we bargain with what dries out on our palms into the air we
breathe? The ghost of all we have lost to the seas roam—until they find
their way to the Nile.

I sit at the reception when the sky goes dark and recite verses from
Al-Burda in whispers. The darkness fades from the face of the sky when I
close my eyes to sing.

MAGHRIB

My heart is the shade of the moon when it's drained of all its shadows.
A few miles down this road, our sadness gets barricaded in pines,
so, everyone would know we are safe here because we have lost someone.
Maami believes extinction is another word for untimely, and I swore
an oath to believe all she does, for I was made in her image,
and her body has the sonograms of all my prayers.
It's the season when ghosts become whisperers
because their absence reminds us of how to live
in the rays of the memories that brighten our rooms,
without having to wake up burning in them.
It's maghrib again—we sit around a white piece of cloth,
the size of grandfather's grave. We are all dressed in white,
and our rosaries are as long as the sleeves of our jellabiya.
I watch my brothers close their eyes, learning to feign their tiredness
in the sound of the Zikir. I sway in silence and listen to the ghosts
of all our dead, giggling in my ears. This circle is the only space
for the men in my house, to cry aloud, even though we believe,
this isn't how to get God's attention.

MIRROR

Blue butterflies trick ants into picking up their eggs
because it mimicked the face of the evening sky.

For the first time, baba was not home
and won't be coming back anytime soon.

I am a boy of seven, and there is a storm brewing in me
but everyone feels it's the hunger.

The imam said I host jinn in my empty stomach.
Then, I begin to see myself differently,

as though in me are layers of makeshift restaurants
held together with the veins of dead soldiers.

Until I can perfect the dilution ratio of tears
to pheromone, no one is moving out of this house.

All the tables are made of a convex mirror.
There is no need to run when it rains,

the ice on the roofs is the sign
of a climate that has tried so much to resist change.

I was afraid the world would end,
a day after the blood moon,

I thought everywhere beyond the kitchen window was
an empty space to bury everyone I love,

so their memories can dangle
from the tree when the wind blows.

THEORY OF AN ALTERNATE COLONY

After Nikki Giovanni

Scars are fluffs on this dark skin,
& like dandelion fruits, they ready us for flight.

It begins with how to keep our lips sealed,
since nothing we say would save us from further theories

of why we took the wrong direction to the sea.
We made it there without our shoes, but we did not lose our legs.

Here, we worship what would keep us alive,
so, we smeared the wall with pheromone ,

to keep track of the things we love
but couldn't keep out of the fire.

Because our home is a hive of broken memories,
not everything chained is enslaved.

We are descendants of shadows on a glistening wall
that encapsulated the widows and their songs.

The newness of widowhood forged phlegm in their throats.
They keep mute as the moon journeys across the south pole.

The taxonomy of the species that lived
in the spaces around where a new colony was built in haste

are enough to want to bring the war to a halt.
At full moon, our wounds shrink smallest,

but this floating colony would not heal from its altitude sickness—
this is the closest we are to the ghosts that loiter in the wind,

waiting to see if we'll hear them instead of the birds.
Everything new needs a name, but this country

must be named by the choughs that hover above our roofs.
A body full of echoes could heal and still sound like a flute in an ebb,

we search for what could be worshipped in the absence of a full moon,
the sky won't be enough. If the rain is how it hears our prayers,

we won't wake to find a pool in our room,
just because we closed our eyes and stayed silent.

EPIPHYTE

The moon had invisible wings
that matched the sky.
It is outstretched, so I know it will rain soon.

As it gets darker,
we learn to sing
with a tongue that scent of a blooming fig.

The moon shines brightest during the curfew,
but it's taboo to read a love note under its reflection.

Mars has more than one moon, and nothing gets lost in it.
The red surface hides the shadows of the wandering birds.

Out of the pulchritude of the soil on which a tree could grow,
I seek a new planet—for what may not survive a day without me.

My brain generates enough electricity to make my body transparent.
In my stomach are sea urchins, their spherical shells tell me that I'm
    alive.

The veins on my hands are telephone wires, lined by crows.
Birds flourish during the war, they fed on the mangoes in the backyard.
There was no time after each burial to climb the tree.
The only time we did was to see how close the fire was to our house.

The birds held firm to the wires when the wind blows.
How many nights does it take them to arrive, do they lose feathers
        on their way here?

There are more birds in the sky during the war.
They fed on the rotten fruits and got their beaks stained

in blood. The ghost of our dead found a home with the birds.
They'll nest their memories where our hands would not reach.

BLUE SIDE OF A BROKEN MIRROR

I once lived   in a room
packed with empty snail shells

and I could only rely on the needle's eye
to predict when next   it would rain

Until my heart stops   being a burden
no matter how big it swells. The men stay

away from the walls, except they stop to push
and they do not cry to the open sky, they fear

it would cost them their erections. Where I come from
the women do not visit the graveyard. On the walls of their rooms

are transition elements, scribbled in oil paints. It's a sign
        the seed would exit
a body how it entered or inverse. Today,
        I learn a new way to look

at my mother. She grew new rib bones   overnight.
Her eyes were ripe mangoes on a rotten stalk that wouldn't fall

no matter the storm. She asked if I saw her face
          the last time I had my back
against the mat in the labor room.   She asked

if I saw the faces   of all my lost friends.
Afraid that my mouth would lose its shape
          if I chisel out a tooth

in protest, I silently fall in love with a room filled
          with ashes. Each time,
I bite my tongue because it reminds me of how
          my own blood tastes,

could it be that nothing gets lost? Maybe the girls squeezed
          through the cracks on the walls,
to make an orphan of their parent's faith,
          hopeful that they may find a new face

from the other side of the broken mirror.
          They got ripped off their names
before they were lowered   into the ground.

I become nameless, even as I walk out of the terminal.
I must let go all my names.

BLOOD MOON

The sky widens its blood vessel   and the moon got stained.
We've lost so much blood here,   nothing else makes the news.

Instead, we give testimonies
about how a girl becomes rile on the face of the moon.

It is not an assembly of dust in the air we breathe.
The girl does not want her child to inherit any of her gowns,

so she sets herself on fire.
Goats were slaughtered to intercede with the sky
        to hold onto the rain

until prayers could blockade the holes
on the roof of the house, where her freedom was exchanged
        for a cow.

When she opens her mouth to laugh at the joke,
she spills her grief all over the tablecloth.

Her stranger husband asks for her health record,
he has heard whispers of how filled she could be with jinn

but no one says anything about the hot air balloons   in her stomach,
or whether it could be digested   to make a glass of her body.

We've lost so much blood here, nothing else makes the news.

NYCTOPHOBIA

In the end,
she mistakes the Arabic word jinn for Janin
and it makes perfect sense,
because both could occur without consent.
She's been in hell for years   and still does not have a scar
to show for it.
Her body was partitioned by armlets
and everywhere in between is a country—a nameless country.
She sometimes fears closing her eyes because she feels her body
would dissolve in the darkness,
and she won't get to show anyone   how
she became a stranger in her own body.
She asks everyone to look into her eyes   . and help
name her after anything they see.
This loss of tongue   is an inheritance she did not bargain for.

WAITING

for Leah Sharibu

It could take a thousand days
to go around the world with a broken wing.

The light that falls from the sky today saves
the footpaths that led the girls away from home.

This world is a ripple beneath a ridge of sand formed by sighs.

I wore a gown made of cobwebs
because everything invisible may grow into a spider.

The air is thick to breathe, and this means there are many ghosts
        in the air.

Grasshoppers eat up the sky in Dapchi, and
the women made horseshoes from the fire.

The horses galloped through the storm
and came back without the riders.

Every step towards the moon is a trap to erase them from the atlas.

The women escaped before the gunshots became audible,
but not the woman whose daughter never returned

because she calls God with a different tongue.

she sat on a stool in the kitchen
waiting for the world to sing her daughter back home

to lead her through the thorns until she finds the footpath
filled with ashes and bullet shells.

She sat mute in the kitchen—waiting
for her daughter's face to pop from the flames.

HOW TO TELL WAR STORIES

Begin with how you don't feel naked these days
even when you are stripped to the skin,
how you think this nightmare about willets will continue.
Imagine how a vulture knows when the horses are thirsty.
If you must tell stories of this war
you must have a scar of your own that only you
know to tell of the pains.
The women did not flee Mosul because they became of wings
overnight. Mosul was evaded by stingers that do not vomit honey,
it led the women through the black kitchen doors
to a snowfield, where they plowed for a season.
The smell of ginger inside the tea reminded them of
what name they had saved for centuries, just for a grandchild.
The people of Maiduguri did not flee their homes,
each body housed a pillar that made up each square meter.
Maiduguri lived in the scalp of their hairs
locked with the clay from the river that flows only in August.
Say nothing about the men and boys, they are either dead or
soon would be. Do not flee because you know how to steer the wind vane,
every war has a similar ending; the survivors will inherit scars
that never heal. The poets do not flee, but their voice boxes become empty.
The children rely on the wind to remind them of how it all started
one quiet morning.

BLACK HOLE

Before I had a tongue
streamlined for dirges,

I lived in a museum
of obsolete memories.

& earned a living,
planting roses

on the graves of dead soldiers.

The black hole
is my uncle's body

pierced by bullets.

It's harmful to talk
of the scars on our dead.

This could be unseen,
or we can assume it is another

of Einstein's prophecy.

How do you differentiate
ghosts from shadows?

For now, I am a pot of azalea or hemp,
or the graftage of both.

Everything that fits inside me
could grow,

that's all you get for trusting me
with the geography of your grief.

Once, I learned Orangutan have
the closest DNA to humans

and sleeps high on a leafy nest.

It was a miracle to have a part of me
that wants to be so high off the ground.

The black hole is the 74 wounds
on the body of an orangutan,

blinded by bullets.
Each hole is a subway

through which the ghosts
of all that won't survive this entropy disappears.

*

Six years after it was rescued
from palm oil workers,

they appeared again on the horizon.

This may be hard to believe,
like a dolphin thirsty inside the ocean,

I crave more space for the eggs
that incubate inside my body.

I want them to grow wings and fly,
if they survive these coming storms.

DOCUMENTARY OF A LOST MAP

I did not know the world could be broken
                    when none of its parts has a spare
Sleep   brings forth everything I owned
Memory   of the day we left home unpacked
The house pillars quivered   before they got torched
My friends became ghosts   even before they got pierced by bullets
I waved, and they did not wave back   I knew something
was wrong   The world was revolving anticlockwise
Or it could be safe to say   the world was moving around a clock
that had stopped working   There is a woman outside the house
She wants to follow us   out of the burning city
She does not remember the route to her old house   after falling
    in love
with the tattoo on a man's forehead   Today   that man lost
    his head
A picture of her missing daughter hangs down
                    her neck like a talisman
She hugged herself when father told her the lines on her palms
                    are too faded to be traced
as would anyone hoping to embrace the solvency of a blurry childhood
I own the memory of this woman   like a toy that meant nothing
                    when it got broken
even though I tried but failed to fix it
                    None of the parts would fit where it fell

ASSEMBLAGE OF STONES FOR A NEW COLONY

I dream of myself hanging on the mast of a sailing vessel / this confirms my sacrifices to this burning country / the charcoal from the ruins will soothe our upset stomach, but how do I swallow it / if I shut my ears / it won't mean the songs stopped playing / here / what I cannot name / I call holy to avoid questioning / I remember days in my father's library / half the books are without the back covers / even though they were written in foreign languages / I knew they were written by dead people / when I think of an angel of death / I only see pictures of myself with bigger front teeth and auricles the shape of cones / the love for those parts of my body that are least sexualized are a form of worship / like hurricanes / praised / because their destructions earn them names that help track our griefs / we are all named after the dead / or what lives but we may outlive / we sought holiness in the strangers we have yet to meet / even though everything holy has a cost / that's how we live until we cannot pay up the debt / for all the fire we made up because we are hungry / and in those moments / we forget what memory it brings along / the fire that makes the sword cannot unmake its memory / of the blood that wets its blade / histories have been unfair to fire / we only hear of what it took from us / and not what it helps to birth / how it made us survive after we stopped mourning / I flirt with my grief and it births memories / of eyes that lost the light in them to the stones in the water / we survive / because we know the fire is as guilty as the water.

BRIEF HISTORY OF THE BODY AS A MAP ON FIRE

I.

Vultures hovered
Over the debris of a resort.

The pool was evidence
it once housed strangers.

I wanted to make music
about the pool, but

I never had
enough water in my mouth.

II.

I took an oath
on a cookbook I found inside the pool.

In it, were recipes
to make soup that'll heal my wounds.

I own a tongue that wears off in prayer,

and a clock that reminds me
of what is no longer alive.

III.

I was born with a mouth
that is a cage, for birds that are extinct.

I don't like to leave home because
I have iridescent scars on my elbows.

I'm nostalgic for what would not fit in my bags
or may suffocate if they do.

Now, I remember I'm in love
with the water, even when I cannot swim.

The scars I inherited are pteryla,
for feathers I learned to sharpen into quills.

The kettle grew bigger as they hovered.
The resort is now a theater of fractured memories.

IV.

There is a kiosk at the end of the street.
It survived the fire,

but everyone says
it's because it is closer to the graveyard.

There is no glory in hunting what borders the dead.

We lived in the graveyard during the war,
it was our best chance at survival.

We embraced what will become of us,
if we let the smoke into our stomachs.

She returned home
a year after we thought she had died

in an accident. We made flutes
from the hollow branches of pawpaw trees

that grow in her backyard.

V.

Because khalwa is the origin of our music,
I ignored the whispers in the night's wind.

Erùpẹ̀ ìdí àmù, kò lè dí ikòkò t' ó fó.
My body is a country founded on salt and stones.

Each morning, I faced the Qibla,

after I washed the soot off my body
and say prayers to the God of dead things.

VI.

The transistor radio brought tales of war
from across the map. Sometimes it ended

with prayers, for the cities that border the ocean
but won't stop burning.

Ọnà ẹ̀rú ló jín, ẹrú náà ní baba.
This country is rooted in shaved goat skins,

or the wings of a nightingale, whose
songs kept the traveler's company.

But everything we don't know how
to love ends up in a cage.

I want someone to love me,
without fastening the edges

of my rib bones with taut strings,
to make a weapon of what needs warmth.

I bask my loneliness in the songs of the birds,
flocking across the resort at night

it became a museum of ghosts,
until we rebuilt the fence from clay.

This hand is a bricolage of what was not lost,
it's all I have that survived burning.

VII.

It takes silence
to fathom what could be made into a song.

Once, a bat got caught in my father's hair,
it stayed for months and hooted in the night.

Soon, his head became a nest,
for pups whose ownership he cannot claim.

I was a bird in my father's hair,
I grew so heavy. He visited the hospital often.

He thought I was dying, but I was only growing,
and I did not plan to leave anytime soon.

I am afraid of the pool.
It takes up the color of the sky at dawn.

I am afraid of what had been lost to the water.

VIII.

I am afraid of losing this tongue to a pool,
I am tired of mourning my friends

who drowned when their prayers were
to walk on water. I am afraid of floating.

It would mean I could get swallowed
by dolphins and be responsible for their deaths.

I am not afraid of death; but I am afraid
of what becomes of the scars left on everyone I loved.

IX.

I am not afraid of loving the scars
on this body, but I am afraid of what smells

of chlorine. I fear the hollowness
in a heart that neither keeps this body floating,

nor echo the songs of the dying birds.
I fear what escaped a cage.

X.

A vulture flaps its wings
over a new cemetery.

Each of its feathers
are maps of countries,

where everyone understands
the language of silence.

When the water in my mouth is enough
to make music, it'll stop the burning.

ACKNOWLEDGMENTS

.I am grateful to the editors and platforms where some of these poems were published, sometimes in different versions.

Tinderbox Poetry Journal: "Genesis" (Nominated for Best New Poet Award)

Salamander Magazine: "Flight", "Satellite Phone Call as a Form of Supplication" (Nominated for Best New Poet Award).

The Cortland Review: "How the War Made Us a Name"

Frontier Poetry: "Aperture Diameter"

Diode Poetry Journal: "Reverse Concert", "Satellite Phone to the Gardener Whose Memory Caught Fire"

The Rumpus: "How to Pray for a Bird in Flight", "Blood Moon"

Blood Orange Review: "Curfew"

Pittsburg Poetry Journal: "Documentary of a Bride in Baptism"

Cream City Review: "Nomenclature"

Rise Up Review: "Hunger"

The Account: A Journal of Poetry, Prose, and Thought: "Reincarnation"

Poet Lore: "Satellite Phone Call to Boys in Faulty Armor Tank"

Anomaly: "Satellite Phone Call to Girls that were Once Sand Miners", "Satellite Phone Call to the Tourist in the Train Station"

Raleigh Review: "Satellite Phone Call to Peace Keepers"

Bayou Magazine: "Wi-Fi in a Cemetery"

Transition Magazine: "Halogen"

Poetry Magazine: Wi-Fi in a Prison Yard"

SAND: "Maghrib"

Waxwing: "Epiphytes"

The Journal: "The Blue Side of a Broken Mirror"

Crab Creek Review: "Waiting"

Cosmonauts Avenue: "How to Tell War Stories"

Magma Poetry: "Documentary of a Lost Map"

Passages North: "Assemblage of Stones for New Colony" (Nominated for Best New Poet Award)

Some of these poems appeared in my chapbook "Harp in a Fireplace".

Thank you to my father, Abdulrasheed Ahmad.

I was nursed by many women; thank you to Hajara and Fatima Abdulrasheed for choosing to understand why I woke up late for breakfast and for keeping me well fed in body and spirit.

Nagode to the league of friends at Purple Art Silver in Kaduna where several of these poems were read in early drafts. Nagode my friend, Eze Ifeanyichukwu Peter for the walk every Sunday night and the many conversations we had on poetry and language.

Thank you to all the generations of poets from Nigeria before me, your works paved the words that made this book. Thank you, Jumoke Verissimo, for that lunch at the University of Ibadan, I remember. Thank you to Kazim Ali and Melissa Ginsburg. Thank you, Okwudili Nebeolisa, for having many gists to brighten up the day. Thank you, Saddiq Dzukogi, for the tuwo we had in Kaduna and the many conversations I won't forget. Thank you, Wale Owoade, and thank you, Salawu Olajide, for reading some earlier drafts from this collection. Thank you to Romeo Oriogun, you inspire many. Thank you, Bola Opaleke, for supporting this dream.

Thank you to Aliyu Mohammed Research Library and Justice Akanbi Library where most poems in this collection were written or edited. Thank you to Jamiu Aweda Ahmad for holding it down even when I littered our room with drafts of the manuscript that became this book. Thank you, Abdulfatai, for listening to my many stories after prayers.

Thank you to the twelve stars: Ahmad, Hauwa, Alabi Agan, Balkiss, Baidoh, Zainab, Khadija, Hassana, Hussaina, Abdullah, Muhammad, and Aminat, for always shining, I love you all!

Thank you to Zainab Omolola Bello.

I have lived through this moment of writing a book in my dreams, and I am grateful for its reality through consistent support from strangers who cheered me through many dark nights. Thank you Janaka for taking a bet on this work and to Carrie and all the editors at Black Ocean Press for believing in me.

Thank you, Kakuri!